complete by **Reading Fundamental**

Reading Leader

Steve Gary Brown ELT Research Center

L101

saramin

Preface

Nobody doubts that reading is one of the most essential tools for obtaining information. People have been reading since the beginning of human history. Good reading skills allow one to interpret ideas more effectively, making reading an important key to success. As the world gets smaller and more connected, finding all the information that we need translated into our native language can be difficult. Therefore, learning foreign languages is becoming increasingly important. English is the most popular language in the world, which is why we need to learn English and learn to read it well. However, reading well is not easy as we'd like it to be. Sometimes we run into unfamiliar cultural references, or encounter unknown words. We may not even be aware of how much of the reading material we truly understand. Reading Leader is designed to help students who are in an EFL (English as a foreign language) environment start reading properly and improve their reading capability as they progress through each level.

The features of Reading Leader are detailed below:

1. A wide variety of topics that are closely related to school curriculum not only help students avoid feeling frustrated by unfamiliar cultural references, but also help build up the confidence to deal with a diversity of subjects.

2. Each book contains word lists of 200-250 words to help you build up your vocabulary skills. That means you'll study 600-750 words for each level, and almost 3000 on completion of the series.

3. You can assess your reading and writing ability through Comprehension Check-Up and Sum Up. Also, since those questions are developed to meet the standards for NEAT (National English Ability Test), students can use this book to competently prepare for NEAT.

We hope that this book and your English knowledge will help you to achieve your future goals.

Steve Gary Brown ELT Research Center

Table of **Contents**

Syllabus

Subject	Title	Word Count	Type	Level of Difficulty	Reading Strategies
UNIT 01 Language & Literature	**Reasons to Keep a Diary**	219	Expository essay	★★	Finding the main idea or topic
UNIT 02 Language & Literature	**Tell Me in a Complete Sentence**	183	Conversation	★★	Identifying time order
UNIT 03 Mathematics	**The Story behind Numbers**	210	Expository essay	★★★	Summarizing & Concluding
UNIT 04 Mathematics	**Birthday Party + More People = Fun!**	211	Diary	★★	Paraphrasing
UNIT 05 Mathematics	**Who Took Away My Pizza?**	216	Lecture	★★	Guessing unknown words in context
UNIT 06 Mathematics	**What Is 1,2,3's Name?**	230	Expository essay	★	Identifying the author's purpose
UNIT 07 Science	**Small but Important, Cells!**	212	Expository essay	★★★★	Understanding details
UNIT 08 Science	**Do You Like Bugs?**	223	Expository essay	★★★★	Summarizing & Concluding
UNIT 09 Science	**Hands Are Not Enough?**	231	Lecture	★★★	Identifying the author's purpose
UNIT 10 History	**Who Was Florence Nightingale?**	215	Biography	★★	Paraphrasing
UNIT 11 History	**The Great Wall of China: The Perfect Travel Adventure**	219	Advertisement	★★★	Understanding details
UNIT 12 History	**China's Greatest Philosopher: Confucius**	218	Presentation	★★★★★	Identifying time order
UNIT 13 Social Studies	**A World of Festivals**	227	Expository essay	★★	Scanning
UNIT 14 Arts	**Let's Draw Different Lines on the Canvas**	223	Miscellaneous essay	★★★	Guessing unknown words in context
UNIT 15 Arts	**Different Tastes in Music**	206	Miscellaneous essay	★	Identifying the author's purpose
UNIT 16 Health & Life	**Is Volleyball Better Than Baseball?**	222	Diary	★★★	Understanding attitude & mood

How to Use This Book

Step 1. Read and Comprehension Check-Up

Each book has 16 Units featuring a wide variety of subjects related to school curriculum. This will ==help you to acquire cultural knowledge and build up the confidence to deal with all types of subjects.== You can also assess your understanding of the reading materials with ==well-developed questions that are compatible with NEAT.==

Step 2. Vocabulary Power-UP

Check the progress of your vocabulary knowledge by matching words in context, understanding the relationship between words, and identifying synonyms using context clues. ==Improve your ability to guess the meaning of unknown words without relying on a dictionary.==

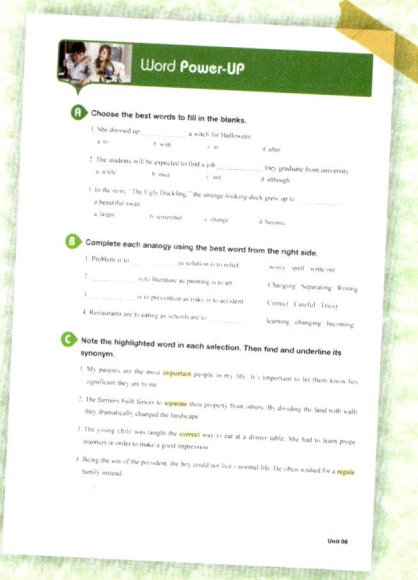

Step 3. Sum UP!

This section gives the reader an insight into how to summarize a passage after reading. This section also provides a variety of writing activities making it helpful when preparing for a writing test or when writing for oneself.

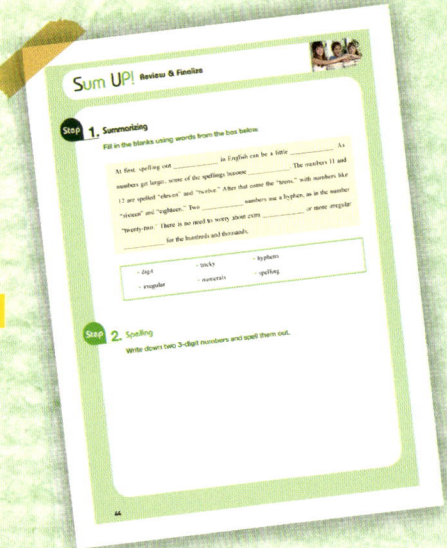

UNIT 01 Reasons to Keep a Diary

1 Warm UP!

- **Think about the following questions.**
  1. How often do you write about your thoughts and feelings?
  2. What would you want to write in your diary?

2 Word Preview

- **Look at the pictures and fill in the blanks with a relevant word from the box below.**

| diary | idea | grandparents | problem | upset |

Reasons to Keep a Diary

Track 01

Reading Strategies

Finding the main idea or topic does not have to be too difficult. What you need to look for is an idea that is not too general, or broad, and not too specific, or narrow. This skill is important when you need a general idea about a passage.

A diary is a book that you write about your own life. You can write about things that happen to you, and how you think about them. There are many reasons that people keep a diary.

How was your day today? Did something exciting happen? Right now your memory of today is fresh. A few months later, however, you may forget much about today. Writing down your activities and thoughts while they are still new will help you to remember them. Years in the future, you can read your diary and remember how your life was and how you were.

Keeping a diary is more than just recording facts. Writing about your ideas and feelings will help you organize your thoughts. If you are upset about a problem, expressing it in words can help you to feel better. It may also help you to think about a problem in a different way. This can help you to solve the problem. Diaries are usually private, but sometimes it is fun to share your story with others. Would you like to know about your grandparent's childhood? If you keep a diary, your children and grandchildren will be able to know more about you. Some people also put their diaries on the Internet. They share their personal stories with thousands of people.

A **Write the best answer.** `for NEAT`

1. What is the topic?

   _____

2. What is one reason to keep a diary?

   _____

B **Check whether the following statements are true or false.**

1. A diary should only contain facts.   True ☐   False ☐

2. Writing in a diary may help you solve problems.   True ☐   False ☐

3. Diaries are private and should never be shared.   True ☐   False ☐

C **Read and choose the best answers.**

1. Which of the following is the reason to keep a diary?
   - a. exercise, make money, use Internet
   - b. remember events, solve problems, share stories
   - c. think more, share stories, know the future
   - d. express oneself, have privacy, forget stories

2. When is not a good time to write a diary?
   - a. after you forgot about the event
   - b. while the memory is still fresh
   - c. when you have a problem to solve
   - d. when you want to express yourself

3. How can keeping a diary help you to solve a problem?
   - a. Your great grandchildren can give you advice.
   - b. The Internet has a lot of useful information.
   - c. Writing will help you remember your problem.
   - d. Writing about it helps you see it from a different perspective.

4. Which of the following is true?   `for NEAT`
   - a. Diaries are for people with exciting lives.
   - b. Anyone can write your diary.
   - c. Diaries are about the people who write them.
   - d. Most people share their diaries.

Word Power-UP

A **Choose the best words to fill in the blanks.**

1. I had a boring day. Nothing interesting _____.

   a. came   b. was   c. kept   d. happened

2. She _____ her vacation on her blog.

   a. thought about   b. owned   c. wrote about   d. put

3. My friend is upset because I _____ her birthday.

   a. shared   b. recorded   c. forgot   d. thought about

4. Reading his old diary brought back memories of his happy _____.

   a. facts   b. problems   c. childhood   d. future

B **Complete each analogy using the best word from the right side.**

1. Parks are to public as houses are to _____.   new shared private

2. Yesterday is to tomorrow as past is to _____.   future grandparents thought

3. Car is to transportation as language is to _____.   excitement expression activities

4. Make is to destroy as _____ is to forget.   organize write remember

C **Note the highlighted word in each selection. Then find and underline its synonym.**

1. My father exercises to keep his body strong. I am impressed by how well he maintains his health.

2. The mechanic couldn't find the reason for the strange sound. The cause of the problem remains a mystery.

3. Librarians carefully organize all the books in the library. In order to find a book it must be arranged properly.

4. He quit his last job due to personal issues. It is too bad his private problems affected his work.

Sum UP! Review & Finalize

 **Step 1. Summarizing**

Fill in the blanks using words from the box below.

A diary is a book that you write about your own _____. Many people

_____ to write about their lives in a diary. There are a _____

of reasons that people do this. Some people _____ reading about and

_____ past events. Expressing one's thoughts in a diary can help people

think about their _____. Some people write so that their children and

_____ can know who they were.

▪ decide	▪ enjoy	▪ grandchildren	▪ life
▪ problems	▪ remembering	▪ variety	

Step 2. Composition `for NEAT`

What did you do today? How did you feel? Write your own diary.

UNIT

02 Tell Me in a Complete Sentence

All things grow with time – except grief.

1 Warm UP!

• **Think about the following questions.**

1. What parts are needed to make a sentence complete?

2. Can you think of an example of a complete sentence?

2 Word Preview

• **Look at the pictures and fill in the blanks with a relevant word from the box below.**

_____ _____ _____ _____ _____

| chocolate | complete | eat | flavor | ice cream |

Tell Me in a Complete Sentence

Track 02

Reading Strategies

Identifying time order Writers often use dates and times, or other words, to show the order of events – for example, first, next, then, later, finally, and today. These words can help you to understand a passage better. Read carefully and identify those words.

Child: Mommy! Ice cream!

Mother: What, dear? What about ice cream?

Child: Ice cream, Mommy! Ice cream!

Mother: I'm sorry, but you'll have to speak in a complete sentence. If you only say "ice cream," I can't be sure what you mean.

Child: I want ice cream!

Mother: Very good. That sentence has a subject and a predicate.

Child: What are a subject and a predicate?

Mother: The subject of a sentence is the person or thing that does an action.

Child: Like eating ice cream?

Mother: Yes. In the sentence, "Jenny eats ice cream," Jenny is the subject. The predicate gives information about the subject. What kind of ice cream do you like?

Child: Chocolate ice cream is delicious.

Mother: Okay. Can you find the predicate in that sentence?

Child: Umm... "is delicious?" But that isn't an action!

Mother: You are correct. Predicates can have verbs that are actions, like "eat ice cream" or "go home," or descriptions, like "is delicious" or "is funny."

Child: I understand. Now, buy me some ice cream!

Mother: Alright. What flavor ice cream do you want?

Child: Chocolate!

Mother: Tell me in a complete sentence.

Child: I would like chocolate ice cream, please.

Mother: Perfect!

Words to Know

action   something that you do

complete   having all of the necessary parts; whole

description   the act of using words to tell others what something is or was like

flavor   the particular way something tastes

predicate   the part of a sentence that tells what the subject does, or what happens to the subject

subject   a noun or noun phrase that is one of the main parts of a sentence. The subject performs the action of the verb or is in the state that the verb phrase describes

verb   a word that is used to say that someone does something or that something happens

Comprehension Check-UP

A **Write the best answer.** for NEAT

1. What is the topic of the conversation?

_____

2. What does a complete sentence need?

_____

B **Check whether the following statements are true or false.**

1. The child doesn't like chocolate ice cream.   True ☐   False ☐

2. The mother wants the child to speak in a complete sentence.   True ☐   False ☐

3. The predicate is the part of the sentence that does the action. True ☐   False ☐

C **Read and choose the best answers.**

1. What is the subject in the sentence, "Mike ate spaghetti at the restaurant"?

   a. Mike   b. ate   c. at the restaurant   d. spaghetti

2. Which of the following is NOT a complete sentence?

   a. I'm fine.   b. What is that?   c. Bought some candy.   d. The cat is black.

3. What is the relationship of the predicate to the subject?

   a. The predicate comes before the subject.

   b. There is no direct relationship between the two.

   c. The predicate describes the subject's condition or action.

   d. The predicate is described by the subject.

4. Which of the following is true? for NEAT

   a. The subject is the action of a sentence.

   b. The mother is concerned about proper grammar.

   c. A sentence can be complete without a verb.

   d. The child doesn't understand grammar.

Word Power-UP

A **Choose the best words to fill in the blanks.**

1. Check your wallet to be _____ you have money.
   a. sure   b. complete   c. good   d. delicious

2. She looked all over but couldn't _____ her cat.
   a. eat   b. have   c. do   d. find

3. The poster included the _____ of her missing cat.
   a. sentence   b. information   c. description   d. kind

4. I didn't think that joke was very _____.
   a. active   b. sure   c. delicious   d. funny

B **Complete each analogy using the best word from the right side.**

1. Comfortable is to furniture as _____ is to food.   chocolate   delicious   like

2. Sports is to _____ as sleep is to relaxation.   action   information   subject

3. Word is to _____ as tomato is to pizza.   predicate   ice cream   sentence

4. Borrow is to lend as take is to _____.   give   eat   act

C **Note the highlighted word in each selection. Then find and underline its synonym.**

1. There are many kinds of restaurants to go to. Just decide what type of food you want to eat.

2. My essay is not quite complete yet. It probably won't be finished until tomorrow.

3. I know you'd like to have more data, but there isn't much information on that subject.

4. Just a single goal was made during the match. That was the only time our team had scored so low.

Step 1. Sentence Completion

Draw a line between A and B to complete each sentence.

A

1. Predicates also contain verbs

2. The next part, the predicate,

3. First, a complete sentence needs

4. What parts are needed

5. This is the person or thing

B

a. gives information about the subject.

b. that does the action.

c. which can be active or descriptive.

d. something called a subject.

e. to make a complete sentence?

Step 2. Sequencing for NEAT

Put the sentences in the correct order.

Making a Complete Sentence

1.

2.

3.

4.

5.

03 The Story behind Numbers

① Warm UP!

• **Think about the following questions.**

1. Do you know where our current number system came from?
2. What did you do today that required using numbers?

② Word Preview

• **Look at the pictures and fill in the blanks with a relevant word from the box below.**

cave	number	Roman numeral	symbol	tally marks

The Story behind Numbers

Track 03

Reading Strategies

Summarizing & Concluding A summary is a restatement of the main points of a paragraph or an article. To summarize a paragraph, you must distinguish more important information from less important information. In other words, you have to ignore the specific details and summarize around a topic or main point. A conclusion is a decision based on several inferences. Conclusion may be either stated or implied.

A number is a symbol that can be used for counting or measuring. You can write a number as a numeral, for example: 1, 2, 3, 4, 5, or you can write a number as a word: one, two, three, four, five. There have been many ways of representing numbers. The most ancient way is called 'tally marks.' People would make lines on cave walls (like ////) to show how much time had passed. With 'tally marks,' however, one could only count, not do complex calculations. During the Roman Empire, people used Roman numerals, where 'V' equaled 5, and 'X' equaled 10. The idea of 'zero' existed in the Indian and Arab world,

but not in Rome. After the Roman Empire ended, a decimal system introduced by Indian and Arab mathematicians became popular. This is the number system most used today, where a zero can represent a 'place,' so that putting a '1' before a '0' means that it is 10 times greater than 1. This makes it easy to do math with large and complex numbers. For example:

$$937$$
$$+\,128$$
$$=1065$$

To do this math using 'tally marks,' we would have to write over a thousand slashes! Thankfully, the Arabic number system has made math, and our lives, easier.

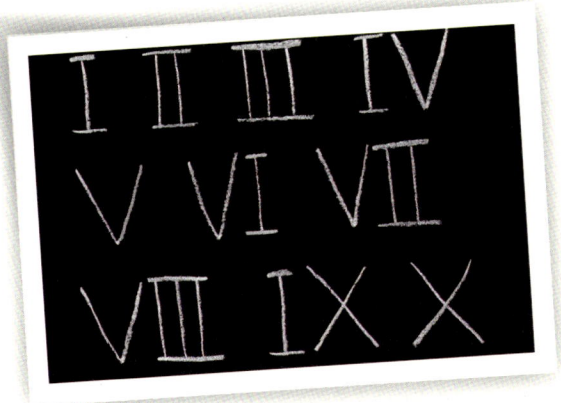

Comprehension Check-UP

A ▶ **Write the best answer.** `for NEAT`

1. What is the topic of the article?

_____

2. Why did number systems change?

_____

B ▶ **Check whether the following statements are true or false.**

1. These days, the Roman numeral system is the most common and useful.

True ☐   False ☐

2. There are many ways to represent numbers.

True ☐   False ☐

3. The idea of 'zero' was invented by Romans.

True ☐   False ☐

C ▶ **Read and choose the best answers.**

1. Which of the following represents the tally marks?
   a. 7   b. VII   c. ///// //   d. seven

2. Which of the following is NOT a Roman numeral?
   a. V   b. X   c. III   d. O

3. What was the greatest contribution of Indian and Arab mathematicians? `for NEAT`
   a. Writing numbers as words   b. The decimal system
   c. The Roman numeral system   d. The tally marks

4. Which of the following is true? `for NEAT`
   a. The Roman numeral for '5' is X.
   b. The tally marks are ideal for complex math.
   c. Newer number systems make math more difficult.
   d. '5' is not a Roman numeral.

Word Power-UP

A ▸ Choose the best words to fill in the blanks.

1. Dinosaurs _____ in the past, but are now all extinct.

   a. measured   b. existed   c. passed   d. were introduced

2. Hot peppers were first _____ in Korea during the 16th century.

   a. introduced   b. equaled   c. popular   d. counted

3. Street signs have _____ on them that tell cars and people what to do.

   a. systems   b. numbers   c. symbols   d. calculations

4. Time _____ quickly when we are having fun.

   a. represents   b. counts   c. introduces   d. passes

B ▸ Complete each analogy using the best word from the right side.

1. Fame is to _____ as money is to rich.   popular   complex   ancient

2. Locomotion is to train as _____ is to computer.   represent   calculator   measure

3. Fat is to thin as modern is to _____.   easy   ancient   popular

4. Scale is to weight as clock is to _____.   time   place   math

C ▸ Note the highlighted word in each selection. Then find and underline its synonym.

1. In order to determine the length of the pants, she measured her legs.

2. In school, her accomplishments equaled those of mine. Our scores were identical in every class.

3. Olympic athletes represent their country when competing abroad. Their success symbolizes glory for their nation of origin.

4. There was no numeral for zero in the Roman Empire. Instead, the symbol for zero came from the Indian and Arab world.

Summarizing [for NEAT]

Complete the diagram with the words from the box below.

Introduction

Throughout history, there have been many ways of _____ numbers. Some number systems are more useful than others.

Example 1

The _____ tally marks were merely simple line markings, and weren't very helpful for making _____.

Example 2

Lacking the concept of _____, the Roman numerals used by the Roman Empire were also limiting.

Reason 3

Indian and Arab mathematicians invented the _____ system, which included the idea of 'zero.'

Conclusion

The _____ number system spread around the world, making _____, and our lives, easier.

▪ ancient	▪ calculations	▪ decimal	▪ Arabic
▪ math	▪ representing	▪ zero	

UNIT
04 Birthday Party + More People = Fun!

1 Warm UP!

- **Think about the following questions.**
  1. Do you like it when many people come to your birthday party?
  2. Are you good at adding up numbers in your head?

2 Word Preview

- **Look at the pictures and fill in the blanks with a relevant word from the box below.**

| birthday cake | birthday party | classmate | present | twins |

UNIT 04
Mathematics

Birthday Party + More People = Fun!

Track 04

Reading Strategies

Paraphrasing When we paraphrase, we take a sentence or passage and use different words to say the same meaning. To understand paraphrasing, we need to make connections between ideas and recognize when different words have the same meaning. Paraphrasing is important in many different kinds of reading questions.

Yesterday my sister Becky had a birthday party. She is two years older than me. I am eight years old, so my sister turned ten [2+8=10]. Her party was lots of fun because so many people came to visit. I think almost twenty people were there to celebrate. Let me add up how many people came to the party. At first it was just our family. There are 2 children, Becky and I, plus my parents, equals 4. Oh, Should I count my dog, too? Let's skip him for now. Then 5 of Becky's classmates came over with cake and presents. That made 9 people [4+5=9]. My uncle and aunt also came over with their twin

babies [2+2=4]. There were four of them, so the total number of people was 13 [9+4=13]. Becky's best friend, Melissa, was traveling with her family so she couldn't make it. If she had been there, there would have been 14 people all together [13+1=14]. I guess there wasn't actually twenty people there. If seven more people had come there would have been that many [13+7=20]. It was a lot of fun, but I hope that even more people come to my birthday party.

Comprehension Check-UP

A Write the best answer. **for NEAT**

1. What is the topic of the article?

_____

2. What was the total number of people at the party?

_____

B Check whether the following statements are true or false.

1. Becky turned ten years old yesterday.   True ☐ False ☐

2. Melissa couldn't come to the party due to illness.   True ☐ False ☐

3. The speaker counted the dog as a party attendee.   True ☐ False ☐

C Read and choose the best answers.

1. Had Melissa been there, what would the total number of people have been?
   a. twenty   b. thirteen   c. fourteen   d. nine

2. Which of the guests brought cake and presents?
   a. their dog   b. Becky's classmates c. their aunt and uncle d. Melissa

3. What was the speaker's predicted number of total guests? **for NEAT**
   a. fourteen   b. thirteen   c. twenty-seven   d. twenty

4. Which of the following is true? **for NEAT**
   a. The speaker is older than Becky.
   b. The speaker wants more people at her party.
   c. Becky wished more people had come.
   d. The speaker is poor at math.

Word Power-UP

A Choose the best words to fill in the blanks.

1. People thought it was strange that Jake wore black clothing _____ every day.
   a. actually   b. total   c. just   d. almost

2. After _____ the price of the meal, they realized that they didn't bring enough money.
   a. visiting   b. adding up   c. making it   d. skipping

3. I wasn't looking forward to the party, but it was _____ a lot of fun.
   a. twin   b. celebrating   c. present   d. actually

4. Even though they are _____, they look quite different from each other.
   a. present   b. total   c. twins   d. almost

B Complete each analogy using the best word from the right side.

1. _____ is to welcoming as guest is to host.   Visiting Traveling Celebrating

2. Payday is to salary as birthday is to _____.   twin total present

3. Joy is to _____ as sadness is to despairing.   counting skipping celebrating

4. Minus is to _____ as less is to more.   add up plus count

C Note the highlighted word in each selection. Then find and underline its synonym.

1. Donna didn't make it to the airport on time. She arrived ten minutes after the plane had taken off.

2. That goal was not considered as a point. It doesn't count because the striker was offside.

3. If you are having trouble answering a question, jump to the next one. Later on, you can go back and work on the problems that you skipped.

4. He had hoped to receive sneakers for his birthday. He never expected that he would get socks instead.

Step 1. Rewriting

Fill in the blanks using words from the box below.

Dear Lisa,

I _____ so many gifts for my birthday this year! I _____ how many
I actually got. Well, my _____ gave me 4 presents, and my younger brother
_____ me 1. Five friends from school also gave me 1 _____ each.
Grandma and grandpa sent a package with 3 presents in it. So, how _____
is that? 4+1=5, and 5+5=10. 10 presents _____ the 3 from my grandparents
makes a total of 13 presents! I wish you could have been there.

Rebecca

• gave	• got	• many	• parents
• plus	• present	• wonder	

Step 2. Composition for NEAT

Reply to the letter as if you were Lisa writing back to Rebecca.

UNIT

05 Who Took Away My Pizza?

1 Warm UP!

- **Think about the following questions.**
  1. What other words do you know that express 'subtraction'?
  2. If you had a pizza, would you want it to be subtracted or added to?

2 Word Preview

- **Look at the pictures and fill in the blanks with a relevant word from the box below.**

    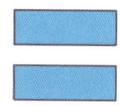

| addition | confusing | equal | opposite | subtraction |

Who Took Away My Pizza?

Track 05

Reading Strategies

Guessing unknown words in context We often meet unknown words while reading a passage. At that time, context gives us an idea of the possible meaning. We can also use our knowledge of how a word is put together to work out its meaning.

Okay, class. So, today we will be talking about 'subtraction.' Subtraction is the opposite of addition. Instead of adding more of something, you take something away. Now, there are various ways to talk about subtraction. Let's say you had five pieces of pizza, and someone ate two of them. That would leave three pieces [5-2=3]. This can be said, "two subtracted from five equals three." Other than 'subtract,' you can also use the words 'minus, less, difference, decrease, take away, or deduct.' For example, five minus two is three. Notice how the word order is different in the two sentences. In the first

example, a number is taken away from the original number. While in the second example, the original number minus another number leaves the answer. Is this confusing? I'll give a few more examples. What is 'ten take away three?' Who knows the answer?

That's right, it's seven [10-3=7]. How about this one? What is 'three less than ten?' Does anybody know?

It's actually the same equation, so the answer is also

seven! Okay, here's another one. There are fifteen students here right now. If tomorrow only nine students show up to class, what is the difference from today? The difference between nine and fifteen is six [15-9=6].

Any questions?

Comprehension Check-UP

A **Write the best answer.** for NEAT

1. What is the topic of the article?

_____

2. How many students are in the class?

_____

B **Check whether the following statements are true or false.**

1. Subtraction is a way to eat pizza.   True ☐   False ☐

2. 'Take away' and 'minus' have the same grammatical usage.   True ☐   False ☐

3. 'Five take away two' is the same as 'two less than five.'   True ☐   False ☐

C **Read and choose the best answers.**

1. Other than 'subtract,' how many words can be used to express 'subtraction'?
   a. none   b. six   c. five   d. seven

2. How does the teacher worry that the students may feel?
   a. hungry   b. easy   c. lonely   d. confused

3. What is the opposite of subtraction?
   a. addition   b. minus   c. deduction   d. attraction

4. Which of the following is true? for NEAT
   a. Seven is ten subtracted from three.
   b. Five take away seven is two.
   c. The difference between eight and four is twelve.
   d. Six minus three is three.

Word Power-UP

A **Choose the best words to fill in the blanks.**

1. Every morning, Mary _____ her cat at home alone while she goes to work.
   a. leaves   b. takes away   c. orders   d. notices

2. Eating the _____ meal day after day becomes boring eventually.
   a. original   b. various   c. opposite   d. same

3. You should _____ the amount of fat in your diet in order to lose weight.
   a. deduct   b. decrease   c. minus   d. leave

4. He is so lazy that he is always putting off things until _____.
   a. something   b. tomorrow   c. only   d. away

B **Complete each analogy using the best word from the right side.**

1. _____ is to diversity as difficulty is to adversity.   Difference Same Original

2. Complexity is to _____ as humor is to funny.   decreasing confusing first

3. Messy is to clean as chaos is to _____.   example opposite order

4. Attention is to _____ as disinterest is to ignoring.   noticing deducting something

C **Note the highlighted word in each selection. Then find and underline its synonym.**

1. We'll know the ==answer== to his medical tests by tomorrow. Let's just hope that the results are positive.

2. Do you know of any cases where a famous athlete was a vegetarian? I can't think of any ==examples== right now.

3. I prefer the first Godfather movie to the others. Most times the ==original== is better than the sequels.

4. I'm sorry, but the owner of the building is ==away== at the moment. She'll probably be gone until this evening.

Step 1. Summarizing

Fill in the blanks using words from the box below.

Subtraction is the opposite of _____, when one amount is taken away from a(n) _____ amount to get an answer. There are many different ways to talk about _____. You can use the words 'minus, less, _____, decrease, take away, or deduct.' _____ on which word you use, the grammar rules change. For example, '7 minus 3 is 4.' Another _____ to say that is 'The difference of 7 and 3 is 4.'

• depending	• difference	• original
• subtraction	• way	• addition

Step 2. Composition [for NEAT]

Give five different ways to write the subtraction problem 10 − 4 = 6.

UNIT
06 What Is 1, 2, 3's Name?

1 Warm UP!

- **Think about the following questions.**
  1. Which numbers are difficult for you to spell?
  2. Do you know which numbers have irregular spellings?

2 Word Preview

- **Look at the pictures and fill in the blanks with a relevant word from the box below.**

_____   _____   _____   _____   _____

Arabic	digit	separate	irregular	regular

What Is 1, 2, 3's Name?

Track 06

Reading Strategies

Identifying the author's purpose When you read a passage, you should try to identify who the author is writing for and what the purpose of writing is. For some writing, like a letter, the audience is usually one person and the purpose of the letter is focused. So the focus of the passage will be different, and readers need to recognize this.

Writing numbers with Arabic numerals, like 1, 2, 3, etc., is easy. Writing these numbers as words in English, however, is a little more difficult. The important thing is correct spelling. Numbers 1 through 10 are written this way: One, two, three, four, five, six, seven, eight, nine, ten. Things get a little tricky after that. As numbers get larger, some of the spellings are irregular. 16 through 19 are easy enough. Just put a "teen" after the original number, and you have sixteen, seventeen, eighteen, and nineteen. The words for 11, 12, and 13 are different. 11 isn't called "one-teen," but rather "eleven." After that is "twelve" and "thirteen." While fourteen is regular, for 15, the "v" in "five" become an "f" to make "fifteen."

With the double digit "-ties" there are also a few irregular spellings. For example, the "l" in twelve changes to an "n" to make "twenty." You need to also be careful spelling 40, which drops the "u," becoming "forty." Remember to use a hyphen separating two digit numbers like 22, written "twenty-two."

Once in the hundreds and thousands, you don't have to worry about hyphens or spelling changes. Just write out the full number using the patterns you've learned. So, a big number like 358,692 is written "three hundred fifty-eight thousand six hundred and ninety-two." Have fun writing the names of your favorite numbers!

Comprehension Check-UP

A **Write the best answer.** for NEAT

1. What is the topic of the article?

_____

2. What kind of number requires a hyphen?

_____

B **Check whether the following statements are true or false.**

1. '5' is an Arabic numeral.   True ☐ False ☐

2. '43' is spelled 'fourty three.'   True ☐ False ☐

3. The spelling of certain numbers is irregular.   True ☐ False ☐

C **Read and choose the best answers.**

1. Which numbers are spelled by putting a "teen" after the original number?
   a. 16, 17, 18   b. 14, 15, 16   c. 11, 12, 13   d. 18, 19, 20

2. Which letter is dropped in the spelling of "40"?
   a. 'y'   b. 'u'   c. 'r'   d. 'o'

3. In which of the following number you don't need to worry about hyphens or spelling changes?
   a. 34   b. 11   c. 40   d. 103

4. Which of the following is true? for NEAT
   a. 14 is spelled fourteen.
   b. All large numbers require a hyphen.
   c. Irregular spelling changes stop after the double digits.
   d. The spelling patterns used for the "teens" are repeated for higher numbers.

Word Power-UP

A ▸ Choose the best words to fill in the blanks.

1. She dressed up _____ a witch for Halloween.

   a. to   b. with   c. as   d. after

2. The students will be expected to find a job _____ they graduate from university.

   a. while   b. once   c. just   d. although

3. In the story "The Ugly Duckling," the strange-looking duck grew up to _____
   a beautiful swan.

   a. larger   b. remember   c. change   d. become

B ▸ Complete each analogy using the best word from the right side.

1. Problem is to _____ as solution is to relief.   worry   spell   write out

2. _____ is to literature as painting is to art.   Changing   Separating   Writing

3. _____ is to prevention as risky is to accident.   Correct   Careful   Tricky

4. Restaurants are to eating as schools are to _____ .   learning   changing   becoming

C ▸ Note the highlighted word in each selection. Then find and underline its synonym.

1. My parents are the most important people in my life. It's important to let them know how
   significant they are to me.

2. The farmers built fences to separate their property from others. By dividing the land with walls,
   they dramatically changed the landscape.

3. The young child was taught the correct way to eat at a dinner table. She had to learn proper
   manners in order to make a good impression.

4. Being the son of the president, the boy could not live a normal life. He often wished for a regular
   family instead.

Sum UP! Review & Finalize

Step 1. Summarizing

Fill in the blanks using words from the box below.

At first, spelling out _____ in English can be a little _____. As numbers get larger, some of the spellings become _____. The numbers 11 and 12 are spelled "eleven" and "twelve." After that come the "teens," with numbers like "sixteen" and "eighteen." Two _____ numbers use a hyphen, as in the number "twenty-two." There is no need to worry about extra _____ or more irregular _____ for the hundreds and thousands.

▪ digit	▪ tricky	▪ hyphens
▪ irregular	▪ numerals	▪ spelling

Step 2. Spelling

Write down two 3-digit numbers and spell them out.

07 Small but Important, Cells!

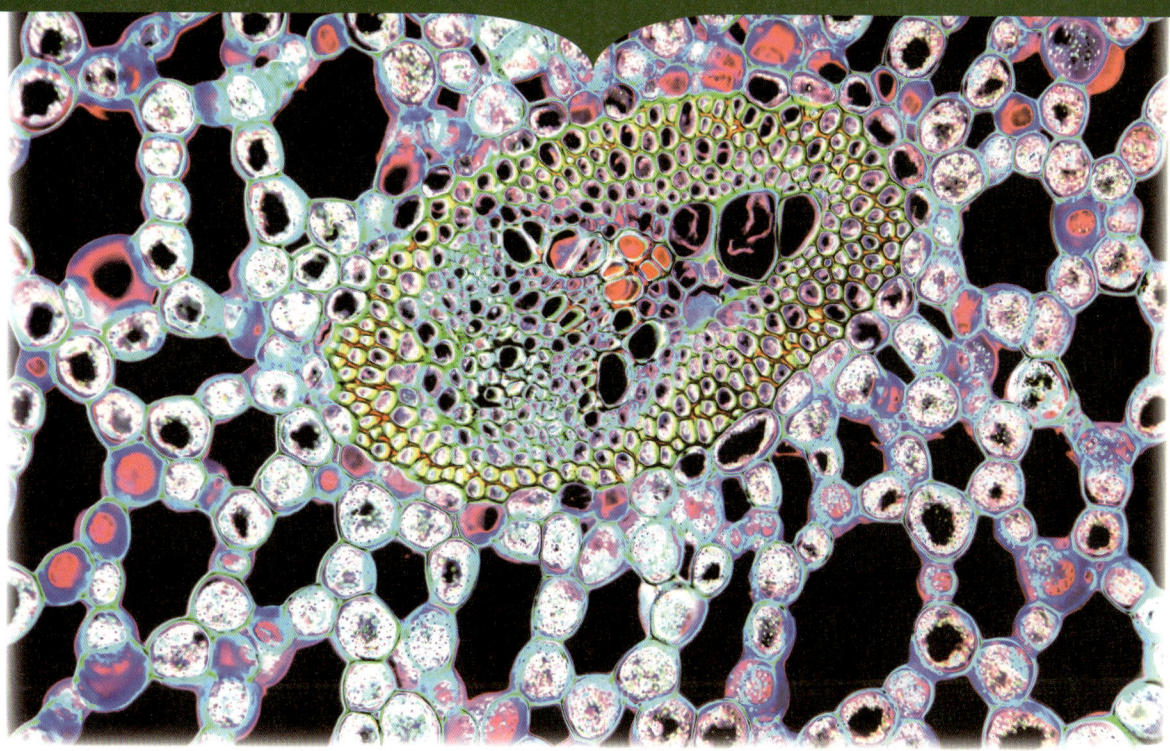

1 Warm UP!

• **Think about the following questions.**
  1. Why is it difficult for us to see most cells?
  2. What is the largest cell in the world?

2 Word Preview

• **Look at the pictures and fill in the blanks with a relevant word from the box below.**

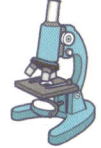  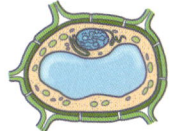 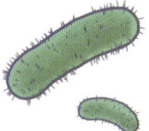 

_____ _____ _____ _____ _____

| ant | bacteria | cell | microscope | ostrich |

Small but Important, Cells!

Reading Strategies

Understanding details Details give readers a better explanation of what the author is trying to say. Details could be used to further describe the topic or to give examples. When dealing with detail questions, only use the information given in the text. Do not imply.

Do you know what the smallest living creature is? You might think it is a mouse, or an ant, but there are living things much smaller than these. Bacteria are single-celled organisms, and they are among the smallest beings. They only have one cell, while mice, ants, and humans have many cells. What is a cell? A cell is like the building block of life. Inside cells are all the tools necessary for life. Why are cells called "cells"? The person who first discovered them through a microscope thought they looked like small rooms. *Cellula* means "small room" in Latin. There are some big cells, however. The largest cell in the world is an ostrich egg! Cells are different in plants and in animals. In complex animals like mice and humans, there are different kinds of cells that have different jobs. Some cells help us to make energy. Some cells help us to fight disease. Other cells have the job for remembering new information. You are using those cells as you read this! The areas where cells work together for a certain job are called "tissues." Muscles

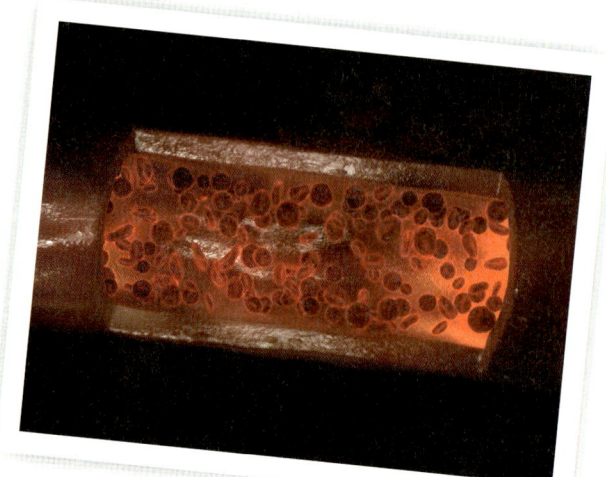

are an example of one type of tissue. Like many members in an organization, cells do various jobs that allow you to live and function.

Comprehension Check-UP

A **Write the best answer.** `for NEAT`

1. What is the topic of the article?

_____

2. How many cells do bacteria have?

_____

B **Check whether the following statements are true or false.**

1. Ants are the smallest living creature.   True ☐   False ☐

2. Cells may have different jobs and functions.   True ☐   False ☐

3. Plants have the same kinds of cells as do animals.   True ☐   False ☐

C **Read and choose the best answers.**

1. Which of the following is something that cells do not do?

   a. help with memory   b. make energy

   c. lay eggs   d. protect us from disease

2. What do we call an area of cells that work together for a common task?

   a. tissue   b. muscle   c. energy   d. organism

3. Why are cells named "cells"?

   a. Because of their complexity

   b. They resemble small rooms.

   c. They are different in plants and in animals.

   d. They work together for a certain job.

4. Which of the following is true?   `for NEAT`

   a. Some cells may live on their own.

   b. Any cell helps us make energy.

   c. Humans have the most cells.

   d. Cells are made up of tissue.

Word Power-UP

A **Choose the best words to fill in the blanks.**

1. He couldn't fix the bicycle because he didn't have his _____.
   a. function   b. energy   c. information   d. tools

2. Summer vacation _____ me time to read lots of books.
   a. discovered   b. allowed   c. thought   d. together

3. Individuals are the _____ of society.
   a. bacteria   b. organisms   c. building blocks   d. tools

4. Many people use machines without understanding how they _____.
   a. function   b. necessary   c. job   d. look like

B **Complete each analogy using the best word from the right side.**

1. Book is to page as house is to _____.   area   room   cell

2. Polar bears are to bears as _____ are to birds.   ants   mice   ostriches

3. Birds are to _____ as bacteria are to simple.   complex   certain   necessary

4. Ancient Chinese is to Korean as _____ is to English.

                                               French   information   Latin

C **Note the highlighted word in each selection. Then find and underline its synonym.**

1. For hours she was unable to find her wallet. She finally discovered it in her couch cushions.

2. I come from the desert region of Africa. There isn't much rain in that area.

3. When you want to grow a garden, some things are essential. Among them, water is very necessary.

4. He is working for an environmental organization. That group is trying to protect our rivers.

Sum UP! Review & Finalize

Step 1. Summarizing

Fill in the blanks using words from the box below.

Cells are tiny building blocks of _____. Some cells, like _____, are independent living beings. Other cells form part of the bodies of _____, animals, and people. Cells contain the _____ necessary for life. They do lots of very important _____, such as making energy and _____ disease. Even though you don't know it, cells are busy working to make you and keep you alive.

▪ bacteria	▪ fighting	▪ jobs
▪ life	▪ plants	▪ tools

Step 2. Composition for NEAT

What are some of the reasons cells are so important?

Subject: Science
Type: Expository essay
Word Count: 223
Level of Difficulty: ★ ★ ★ ★

08 Do You Like Bugs?

1 Warm UP!

- **Think about the following questions.**
  1. What kind of insect do you think is scary?
  2. How do bugs help us and our planet?

2 Word Preview

- **Look at the pictures and fill in the blanks with a relevant word from the box below.**

| bee | glacier | mite | scorpion | spider |

Do You Like Bugs?

Track 08

Reading Strategies

Summarizing & Concluding A summary is a restatement of the main points of a paragraph or an article. To summarize a paragraph, you must distinguish more important information from less important information. In other words, you have to ignore the specific details and summarize around a topic or main point. A conclusion is a decision based on several inferences. Conclusion may be either stated or implied.

There is a lot of confusion about insects. Do you know that spiders are not insects? Neither are scorpions or mites. To be an insect, you must have three body segments, six legs, and antennae. Spiders have two body segments and eight legs. Maybe you think insects are not useful. I used to think insects were gross. To me, bugs were creepy crawling little monsters. Bugs were dirty, dangerous, and annoying. I used to wish that all the bugs on the earth would disappear. But then one day I found a book that explains how important insects are.

In fact, it turns out that we need insects much more than they need us! One way that insects help us is by pollinating plants. Bees, for example, take the pollen from flowers and spread it to others. This allows plants, including the vegetables we eat, to reproduce. Another useful job of insects is to eat and get rid of dead matter. Dead plants and animals are "cleaned up" by lots of hard-working insects. The more I learned about insects, the more interesting they became. There are more than a million kinds of insects in the world. Some insects can live in extreme places, like in a volcano or a glacier. I hope that you will respect insects for the amazing animals that they are.

Comprehension Check-UP

A ▶ **Write the best answer.** `for NEAT`

1. What is the topic of the article?

   _____

2. How many legs do insects have?

   _____

B ▶ **Check whether the following statements are true or false.**

1. Insects need humans to survive.   True ☐ False ☐

2. The author thinks that insects are gross.   True ☐ False ☐

3. The world would be better without bugs.   True ☐ False ☐

C ▶ **Read and choose the best answers.**

1. Which of the following is something that insects do not do?

   a. make webs to catch food   b. help pollinate plants

   c. live in extreme conditions   d. clean up dead matter

2. Which is NOT a characteristic of insects?

   a. six legs   b. two body segments   c. antennae   d. hard-working

3. Why did the author change her mind about insects?

   a. There is a lot of confusion about insects.

   b. She was bothered a lot by bugs before.

   c. Insects helped the author a lot.

   d. She read a book about how useful insects were.

4. Which of the following is true? `for NEAT`

   a. Insects are dangerous to most plants.

   b. There are over a million types of bugs.

   c. Insects only live in comfortable places.

   d. Some insects have eight legs.

Word Power-UP

A **Choose the best words to fill in the blanks.**

1. The children tried to _____ the broken glass before their parents got home.
   a. allow　　　　　b. annoy　　　　　c. get rid of　　　　d. crawl

2. It _____ that we don't have a test today after all.
   a. turns out　　　b. explains　　　c. is cleaned up　　d. spreads

3. During the spring, all the _____ in the air gives Jenny allergies.
   a. millions　　　b. body segments　c. birds　　　　　d. pollen

4. He had to _____ to his teacher why he was late to class.
   a. reproduce　　b. explain　　　c. clean up　　　　d. respect

B **Complete each analogy using the best word from the right side.**

1. Apple is to fruit as cucumber is to _____.　　vegetable plant pollen

2. Babies are to _____ as birds are to flying.　　hard-working dirty crawling

3. Whiskers are to cats as _____ are to ants.　　antennae segments bodies

4. Mountain is to stone as _____ is to ice.　　volcano glacier dirty

C **Note the highlighted word in each selection. Then find and underline its synonym.**

1. The toy train had a number of <mark>segments</mark>. After connecting all the different parts, they put it on the track.

2. My mother is the most <mark>hard-working</mark> person I know. I wish I were as diligent as she is.

3. With a puff of smoke, the wizard vanished. Harry Potter stared at the place where the man had <mark>disappeared</mark>.

4. I thought that my brother was irritating enough by himself. When his <mark>annoying</mark> friends came over, it was even worse.

Summarizing for NEAT

Complete the diagram with the words from the box below.

Introduction

Many people think that insects are _____ or scary. The truth is, however, that bugs are more interesting and _____ than I ever realized.

Supporting Statement 1

Bees and other insects spread the _____ of plants around, so that flowers, fruits and vegetables will grow.

Supporting Statement 2

Other insects _____ organic matter waste. They basically help clean up dead plants and animals.

Supporting Statement 3

Insects are also surprisingly _____! Some bugs can survive extreme _____ and temperature.

Conclusion

In reality, it seems, we _____ insects more than they need us!

• conditions	• tough	• gross	• need
• pollen	• remove	• useful	

UNIT

09 Hands Are Not Enough?

1 Warm UP!

- **Think about the following questions.**
  1. What kinds of tools do you have in your house?
  2. What tool is the most important to you?

2 Word Preview

- **Look at the pictures and fill in the blanks with a relevant word from the box below.**

  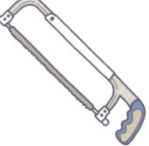  

_____ _____ _____ _____ _____

| hammer | pollution | saw | screwdriver | stick |

Hands Are Not Enough?

Track 09

Reading Strategies

Identifying the author's purpose When you read a passage, you should try to identify who the author is writing for and what the purpose of writing is. For some writing, like a letter, the audience is usually one person and the purpose of the letter is focused. So the focus of the passage will be different, and readers need to recognize this.

What if we had to do everything with our bare hands? Life would be very difficult and uncomfortable. Luckily we have tools. Tools are instruments that help people to do a certain task. Activities would be much harder to do without such tools. Common tools today are hammers, saws, and screwdrivers. The first tools were probably sticks and stones. People used them to hunt animals and to build houses. For thousands of years, humans have been using tools in order to shape their environment. People used to think that only humans use tools. In fact, some monkeys use sticks and stones to reach and eat food. They even teach their children how to use the tools! The ability to create and use tools is also called 'technology.' As people learned more about their world, technology improved. People created

tools that helped them to farm, mine, and build large buildings. Eventually, machines were developed. Machines are devices that use energy to work. They are able to do many things that humans can't. Many good things have happened because of tools and machines, but there are also some bad parts to technology. Many machines damage the air and water with pollution. Trees and animals are also disappearing. These days, technology is developing very quickly. The world may soon be transformed again. Do you think that it will be a better world than now?

bare uncovered or without clothing; naked

damage harm or injury that makes something less useful or valuable

eventually in the end, especially after a long time

instrument a device used for a specific purpose

mine to dig in the earth for minerals such as gold or coal; to work in a mine

reach to touch or take hold of something by stretching out part of the body toward it

technology scientific knowledge or equipment that is used to accomplish something

transform to change the form, look, or shape of

in order to for the purpose of; so that

what if what would happen if

Comprehension Check-UP

A **Write the best answer.** `for NEAT`

1. What is the topic of the article?

_____

2. What were most likely the first tools?

_____

B **Check whether the following statements are true or false.**

1. Some animals can use tools.   True ☐   False ☐

2. Tools require energy to work.   True ☐   False ☐

3. Humans have used tools for hundreds of years.   True ☐   False ☐

C **Read and choose the best answers.**

1. Which of the following are all machines?

   a. hammer, knife, stick   b. stereo, car, telephone

   c. elevator, toaster, shovel   d. refrigerator, fork, computer

2. Which activity does not require any tools?

   a. driving   b. gardening   c. cooking   d. shaking hands

3. What makes a machine different from a tool?

   a. Machines require energy to run.

   b. Tools are not as expensive.

   c. Monkeys can't use machines.

   d. Machines are better for the environment.

4. Which of the following is true? `for NEAT`

   a. Nature has been damaged by technology.

   b. Life is easier without tools.

   c. Animals are unable to use tools.

   d. Machines have only done good things.

Word **Power-UP**

(A) Choose the best words to fill in the blanks.

1. My friend taught me _____ say 'hello' in Japanese.
   a. reach   b. how to   c. use to   d. common

2. The family hasn't decided what name to _____ their new puppy.
   a. reach   b. create   c. shape   d. call

3. Sally couldn't _____ the cereal, so she asked her brother to help her.
   a. transform   b. reach   c. hunt   d. saw

4. It is _____ to some people to sit cross-legged for a long period of time.
   a. uncomfortable   b. lucky   c. technological   d. common

(B) Complete each analogy using the best word from the right side.

1. _____ is to a sculptor as words are to a poet.   Stone Stick Screwdriver

2. Bananas are to _____ as fish is to cats.   farming hands monkeys

3. Guns are to _____ as tractors are to farming.   mining hunting building

4. Crumbs are to bread as _____ are to trees.   sticks air tools

(C) Note the highlighted word in each selection. Then find and underline its synonym.

1. When the power went off in our house, we used batteries to provide energy.

2. In art class, the children learned to mold pieces of clay. Jimmy shaped his clay into a snake.

3. I didn't know you had the ability to speak Spanish. What a useful skill to have!

4. Years of exposure to rain has damaged the sculpture. It has deteriorated a lot.

Step 1. Summarizing

Fill in the blanks using words from the box below.

Humans _____ tools in order to make life easier and better. The early tools were basic, like sticks and _____, but slowly tool-making _____. As tool _____ advanced, people changed their environment to meet their needs. Eventually, very powerful _____ were developed. While these machines make life more _____, they also have a negative effect on the health of the _____.

▪ convenient	▪ environment	▪ improved	▪ invented
▪ machines	▪ stones	▪ technology	

Step 2. Composition for NEAT

How do you use tools in your daily life?

10 Who Was Florence Nightingale?

1 Warm UP!

- **Think about the following questions.**
  1. What would you like to do to help other people?
  2. Do you think girls are just as smart as boys?

2 Word Preview

- **Look at the pictures and fill in the blanks with a relevant word from the box below.**

| graph | lamp | nurse | patient | soldier |

Who Was Florence Nightingale?

Track 10

Reading Strategies

Paraphrasing When we paraphrase, we take a sentence or passage and use different words to say the same meaning. To understand paraphrasing, we need to make connections between ideas and recognize when different words have the same meaning. Paraphrasing is important in many different kinds of reading questions.

Have you heard of a woman named 'Florence Nightingale'? She is famous for her contributions to science, medicine, and the social progress of women. She was born into a wealthy British family in 1820. She was named 'Florence' because she was born in Florence, Italy. At that time very few women were allowed to go to school. Florence's father, however, taught her many things. She learned math, science, philosophy, and foreign languages. Even though her family was rich, she wanted to study to become a nurse. At first her

family didn't like this, but eventually she went to Germany to study. When the Crimean War began, Florence went to Turkey to work as a nurse for wounded soldiers. She was known as "The Lady with the Lamp" because she would walk around the hospital at night, checking on patients with a lamp in hand. She found that the hospital conditions were very bad. Because of these bad conditions, more people were dying from disease than from battle wounds. Florence was skilled at statistics, or measuring and presenting information. She carefully gathered information and made graphs to explain her findings. Her work convinced the military to change the way they ran the hospital. Her new system saved many lives, and made her famous around the world.

Comprehension Check-UP

A **Write the best answer.** `for NEAT`

1. What is the topic of the article?

_____

2. What is Florence Nightingale famous for?

_____

B **Check whether the following statements are true or false.**

1. Florence was born in Germany.   True ☐   False ☐

2. Florence's family wanted her to be a nurse.   True ☐   False ☐

3. In Florence's time, many women did not get an education.   True ☐   False ☐

C **Read and choose the best answers.**

1. Which of the following were abilities that Florence had?

   a. philosophy, cooking, measuring

   b. statistics, science, nursing

   c. aviation, making graphs, convincing

   d. foreign languages, nursing, military leadership

2. Which of the following is Florence not famous for?

   a. medicine   b. literature   c. science   d. women's rights

3. What was the greatest cause of death to soldiers during the Crimean War?

   a. Wounds from the battle field   b. Poor hospital conditions

   c. Lack of medical care   d. Military mistakes

4. Which of the following is true? `for NEAT`

   a. Lamps were dangerous to have in hospitals.

   b. Florence was a brave soldier.

   c. Florence came from a poor family.

   d. Skill at statistics has helped to save lives.

Word Power-UP

A **Choose the best words to fill in the blanks.**

1. The invention of *Hangul* was perhaps King Sejong's greatest _____ to his subjects.
   a. progress   b. soldier   c. measure   d. contribution

2. The mother went to _____ the baby after hearing it crying.
   a. be skilled at   b. check on   c. convince   d. run

3. Even though it took a very long time, they _____ finished the marathon.
   a. never   b. were known as   c. eventually   d. allowed

B **Complete each analogy using the best word from the right side.**

1. Aristotle is to _____ as Freud is to psychology.   progress presenting philosophy

2. Waiters are to customers as doctors are to _____.   patients hospitals medicine

3. Wet is to water as _____ is to Michael Jackson.   social famous measure

4. _____ are to light as batteries are to energy.   Nurses Lamps Graphs

C **Note the highlighted word in each selection. Then find and underline its synonym.**

1. I knew that she was skilled at playing the piano, but I didn't realize that she was also adept at martial arts.

2. Incredibly, she runs the business all by herself. It seems like too much for one person to operate.

3. Bob was convinced that aliens exist. He couldn't be persuaded to think otherwise.

4. The teacher was impressed by the student's rapid progress. He wondered what had caused such an improvement.

1. Rewriting

Fill in the blanks using words from the box below.

Dear John,

Remember how you said that I couldn't be a _____ because I was a

_____? Not only was that a mean thing to say, it was also very mistaken.

There have been many women who made important _____ to science.

One of my _____ is Florence Nightingale. Her work made hospitals

_____ and _____ more effective. Therefore, you should stop

saying things that are mean and _____.

                                                                                    Betty

• contributions	• girl	• heroes	• medicine
• safer	• scientist	• untrue	

2. Composition `for NEAT`

Reply to the letter as if you were John writing back to Betty.

UNIT

11 The Great Wall of China: The Perfect Travel Adventure

1 Warm UP!

- **Think about the following questions.**
  1. Do you know why the Great Wall of China is so famous?
  2. Why do you think the Great Wall was built?

2 Word Preview

- **Look at the pictures and fill in the blanks with a relevant word from the box below.**

| brick | desert | dirt | landmark | plateau |

The Great Wall of China: The Perfect Travel Adventure

Track 11

Reading Strategies

Understanding details Details give readers a better explanation of what the author is trying to say. Details could be used to further describe the topic or to give examples. When dealing with detail questions, only use the information given in the text. Do not imply.

Can you imagine a trip to China without visiting its most famous landmark? You have heard about the Great Wall, but how much do you really know about it?

Why was the wall built?

The Great Wall was begun by Emperor Qin, the king who connected all the individual states of China, in order to protect the country from attack by northern tribes.

What was the wall built from?

Dirt, brick, and people! At first it was built with earth and mud, but during the Ming dynasty it was constructed of bricks. So many people worked to build the wall. Construction was very difficult, and up to 1 million people died while working on it. Many of them were buried inside the wall itself.

Fun facts!

Did you know?

The Great Wall of China is not really one wall, but many parts spread throughout China. The Great Wall's construction began two thousand years ago, but has been expanded and rebuilt numerous times. The Great Wall stretches over 6,400km across mountains, plateaus, and deserts.

A trip to the Great Wall of China is rewarding in many ways: an education in history, an experience of human achievement, and an unforgettable sight.

Pack your bags and grab your camera and come see the Great Wall of China for yourself!

Comprehension **Check-UP**

A Write the best answer. `for NEAT`

1. What is the topic of the article?

_____

2. What does this advertisement want the reader to do?

_____

B Check whether the following statements are true or false.

1. The Great Wall of China was built to provide a great travel adventure.

   True ☐   False ☐

2. The Great Wall consists of many different walls.

   True ☐   False ☐

3. Tourists who visit the wall need protection from northern invaders.   True ☐   False ☐

C Read and choose the best answers.

1. Which of the following is the Great Wall not constructed of?

   a. mud   b. people   c. ceramic   d. bricks

2. What did Emperor Qin succeed in doing?

   a. Kill around one-million people

   b. Complete the Great Wall of China

   c. Unite the warring states of China

   d. Stop attacks from northern invaders

3. Which of the following is true? `for NEAT`

   a. Northern invaders killed one million workers.

   b. The function of the Great Wall has changed in time.

   c. The Qin dynasty used bricks to construct the wall.

   d. Construction on the wall stopped two thousand years ago.

Word Power-UP

A Choose the best words to fill in the blanks.

1. As the number of customers grew, the restaurant _____ to make more room.
   a. buried   b. was begun   c. expanded   d. heard

2. The old clock tower is the main _____ in the small town.
   a. landmark   b. travel   c. plateau   d. dynasty

3. You should think _____ yourself and don't let others tell you what to do.
   a. for   b. with   c. out of   d. up to

4. Mike's mother _____ him a sandwich and a salad for lunch today.
   a. protected   b. built   c. packed   d. connected

B Complete each analogy using the best word from the right side.

1. _____ are to containers as computers are to electronics.

   Bags   Cameras   Landmarks

2. A chief is to a _____ as a mayor is to a city.

   wall   tribe   trip

3. _____ are to science as food is to cooking.

   Individuals   Sights   Facts

4. A library is to books as a _____ is to sand.

   desert   dynasty   dirt

C Note the highlighted word in each selection. Then find and underline its synonym.

1. The Internet helps connect us with other people. I can link my website to those of my friends.

2. After finishing his long journey, he spent some time thinking and writing about his travels.

3. Looking at the view of her town from the hot air balloon, she knew she wouldn't forget the sight.

4. In soccer, the goalkeeper's job is to defend the goal. He may even use his hands to protect the goal.

Step 1. Summarizing

Fill in the blanks using words from the box below.

The Great Wall of China is one of the world's most famous _____. It was _____ built two thousand years ago to keep _____ out of the kingdom. There is actually not one single _____, but many walls stretching 6,400 _____ long. They have been built and rebuilt by different _____ throughout the years. These days, the Great Wall is an iconic monument and a popular travel _____.

• dynasties	• destination	• invaders	• kilometers
• originally	• wall	• wonders	

Step 2. Composition for NEAT

Why is the Great Wall of China such a popular travel destination?

12 China's Greatest Philosopher: Confucius

1 Warm UP!

- **Think about the following questions.**
  1. Do you know about the philosophy of Confucius?
  2. In what countries were Confucius's ideas most influential?

2 Word Preview

- **Look at the pictures and fill in the blanks with a relevant word from the box below.**

"Remember, no matter where you go, there you are. Confucius"

chaos	elder	noble	presentation	quote

China's Greatest Philosopher: Confucius

Track 12

Reading Strategies

Identifying time order Writers often use dates and times, or other words, to show the order of events – for example, first, next, then, later, finally, and today. These words can help you to understand a passage better. Read carefully and identify those words.

Hello, everyone. Today I will give a presentation about Confucius. Confucius was a philosopher in ancient China, around 500 BC. At that time, there were many wars and chaos in China. Confucius thought that if society was well-organized and government was good, then life would be peaceful. His main idea was that people should do their proper duty, and care more about society than their own desires. What is doing one's proper duty? Well, one example is being loyal to one's family and government. Children should respect elders, and citizens should obey their leaders.

Confucius believed that education was very important for individuals and society. When the government in China decided to use his philosophy, it changed the way that schooling and government worked. Originally, only those from rich and noble families could get power

and join government. Confucius put more importance on merit, or ability, so that a poor person who works and studies hard could also succeed. Confucianism has spread and become an important part of the cultures of China, Korea, Japan, and other parts of the world.

I would like to finish with a quote by Confucius,

"Choose a job you love, and you will never have to work a day in your life."

Thank you for your time, I hope you enjoyed my presentation.

Comprehension Check-UP

A Write the best answer. for NEAT

1. What is the topic of the article?

_____

2. When did Confucius live?

_____

B Check whether the following statements are true or false.

1. Confucius went to Japan and Korea to spread his philosophy.   True ☐ False ☐

2. Confucius lived in a time of great social chaos.   True ☐ False ☐

3. Confucius was an individualist.   True ☐ False ☐

Read and choose the best answers.

C

1. Which of the following is an accomplishment of Confucius? for NEAT

   a. He never had to work a day in his life.

   b. He brought peace and order to ancient China.

   c. He helped to establish a merit-based education system.

   d. He persuaded elders to respect children more.

2. Which of the following was NOT a subject of Confucian philosophy?

   a. duty   b. government   c. education   d. English

3. What does a merit-based education system mean?

   a. Bad students were punished with merits.

   b. One's ability matters more than one's wealth.

   c. Poor students are given special attention at school.

   d. Students must obey their teachers.

4. Which of the following is true? for NEAT

   a. Confucius was a powerful member of government.

   b. Few people know who Confucius is.

   c. Confucius thought more about society's needs than his own.

   d. After Confucius, only rich people were able to attend school.

Word Power-UP

A ▶ Choose the best words to fill in the blanks.

1. I didn't understand some of the test questions because I missed last week's _____ on the topic.
   a. philosopher   b. education   c. presentation   d. chaos

2. Due to Columbus's voyage, the Spanish brought their _____ to the America.
   a. ability   b. success   c. desires   d. culture

3. Rather than fighting, you should find a _____ way to solve your problems.
   a. peaceful   b. elder   c. ancient   d. hard

4. People cover their mouths when they cough so that the disease does not _____.
   a. organize   b. join   c. spread   d. proper

B ▶ Complete each analogy using the best word from the right side.

1. Battles are to _____ as innings are to games.   peacetime wars power

2. Plato is to _____ as Mozart is to composer.   philosopher presenter poet

3. School is to _____ as airport is to transportation.   culture individuals education

4. _____ is to order as day is to night.   Chaos Organize Government

C ▶ Note the highlighted word in each selection. Then find and underline its synonym.

1. The dirt road led to an ==ancient== forest. The trees there were very old and big.

2. The Siamese twins were born ==joined== at the hip. They remained connected until they could be separated.

3. She studies many things, but her primary subject is astronomy. Finding out about the universe is her ==main== goal.

4. He has too many wants. Someone who ==desires== so much will end up disappointed.

Sum UP! Review & Finalize

Step 1. Sentence Completion

Draw a line between A and B to complete each sentence.

A

1. Confucianism has spread

2. This merit-based philosophy

3. He valued merit, or ability,

4. Confucius was a philosopher

5. Even in modern-day Korea

B

a. more than one's rank in society.

b. in ancient China, around 500 BC.

c. promoted a greater access to education.

d. his ideas remain very influential.

e. to many parts of the world.

Step 2. Sequencing for NEAT

Put the sentences in the correct order.

China's Greatest Philosopher: Confucius

1. _____

2. _____

3. _____

4. _____

5. _____

UNIT
13 A World of Festivals

1 Warm UP!

- **Think about the following questions.**
  1. What kind of festival is popular in your country?
  2. If you could make a festival, what kinds of activities would you want to happen?

2 Word Preview

- **Look at the pictures and fill in the blanks with a relevant word from the box below.**

| religious | costume | crowd | festival | sculpture |

UNIT 13
Social Studies

A World of Festivals

Track 13

Reading Strategies

Scanning Scanning is used to find a particular piece of information. Run your eyes over the text looking for the specific piece of information you need. Use scanning on schedules, meeting plans, etc. in order to find the specific details you require. If you see words or phrases that you don't understand, don't worry when scanning.

What kind of festivals have you been to? A festival is kind of like a big party. It usually is a celebration of something interesting or important to people. There are many different kinds of festivals: music festivals, food festivals, religious festivals; all sorts of festivals. Some examples of famous festivals are: "La Tomatina" in Spain, "Octoberfest" in Germany, and "Burning Man" in the United States. During La Tomatina, 30,000 people gather and hold the world's biggest food fight. There are no rules and no purpose except to enjoy throwing tomatoes. If you are more a meat and beer person than a tomato lover, then Octoberfest is the festival for you. Millions of beer drinkers head to Germany to eat sausage, chicken, and drink Munich's famous beer. One of the most bizarre festivals is Burning Man, where people build a temporary city in the desert, dress in strange costumes, and make artistic sculptures. Other festivals include Woodstock in New York state, where famous musicians play music to large crowds for days. Texas's Spamarama celebrates and mocks spam, not by eating it, but by building sculptures out of it. In Phuket, Thailand, there is a "Vegetarian Festival" where some people stick sharp objects through their cheeks and tongue! Which festival would you like to go to? If you could start your own festival, what would it be about?

Comprehension Check-UP

A ▸ Write the best answer. [for NEAT]

1. What is the topic of the article?

_____

2. Where is the Burning Man festival held?

_____

B ▸ Check whether the following statements are true or false.

1. Spamarama is for people who like to eat spam. True ☐ False ☐

2. La Tomatina doesn't have any rules. True ☐ False ☐

3. Burning Man is a celebration of music. True ☐ False ☐

C ▸ Read and choose the best answers.

1. Which of the following festival is about food fighting? [for NEAT]
   a. Spamarama   b. Octoberfest   c. La Tomatina   d. Phuket's Vegetarian Festival

2. Who would most likely NOT enjoy Octoberfest?
   a. a German   b. a musician   c. an artist   d. a vegetarian

3. What makes La Tomatina and Spamarama different from Octoberfest?
   a. They both involved food fights.
   b. They are both based in Europe.
   c. They both play with food instead of eating it.
   d. They have more people attending the festivals.

4. Which of the following is true? [for NEAT]
   a. People should dress formal for La Tomatina.
   b. Most festivals are religious.
   c. Munich is famous for its music.
   d. Octoberfest has over a million attendees.

Word Power-UP

A **Choose the best words to fill in the blanks.**

1. You should be careful when handling _____ knives.
   a. bizarre   b. interesting   c. stick   d. sharp

2. If somebody _____ you, it is best to ignore them and not to get upset.
   a. throws   b. mocks   c. sorts   d. enjoys

3. I have seen some strange costumes before, but that is the most _____ costume I have ever seen.
   a. religious   b. famous   c. important   d. bizarre

4. She took the pile of clay and made a bowl _____.
   a. out of it   b. through it   c. during it   d. to hold it

B **Complete each analogy using the best word from the right side.**

1. Instruments are to _____ as balls are to athletes.   musicians celebrations lovers

2. _____ is to wood as melting is to ice.   Burning Sticking Throwing

3. _____ are to spaghetti sauce as soy beans are to soy sauce.

   Sausages Vegetarians Tomatoes

4. Academic is to universities as _____ is to mosques.

   important religious famous

C **Note the highlighted word in each selection. Then find and underline its synonym.**

1. Have you played the ball toss game? Just throw the ball into the basket for a prize.

2. She doesn't like being in large crowds, so she avoids events that draw masses of people.

3. To transfer the file, stick the USB into the computer. So as not to damage it, be careful to insert it carefully.

Step 1. Outlining

Fill in the blanks using words from the box below.

Name of Festival	Location	Main Activity
1. La Tomantina •	a. Texas •	① People stick sharp things in their _____.
2. Octoberfest •	b. Spain •	② Building _____ out of Spam
3. Burning Man •	c. New York •	③ Days of _____ by famous musicians
4. Woodstock •	d. Thailand •	④ World's biggest food _____ with tomatoes
5. Spamarama •	e. Germany •	⑤ Drinking lots of _____ and eating lots of meat
6. Vegetarian Festival •	f. United States •	⑥ Build an artistic city in the _____

▪ beer	▪ concerts	▪ desert
▪ fight	▪ mouths	▪ sculptures

Step 2. Matching

Draw a line matching the name of the festival with the correct location and main activity in the chart.

UNIT 14
Let's Draw Different Lines on the Canvas

1 Warm UP!

- **Think about the following questions.**
  1. Is it easy for you to draw a straight line?
  2. When sending a text message, what kinds of lines can you use to express emotion?

2 Word Preview

- **Look at the pictures and fill in the blanks with a relevant word from the box below.**

| curvy | horizontal | slanted | triangle | vertical |

Let's Draw Different Lines on the Canvas

Track 14

Reading Strategies

Guessing unknown words in context We often meet unknown words while reading a passage. At that time, context gives us an idea of the possible meaning. We can also use our knowledge of how a word is put together to work out its meaning.

I like to draw. When I draw, the first thing I start with is a line. A line is basically two points that are connected. A line can look many different ways. It can go in different directions, and it can have different sizes. What types of lines are there?

A straight line has no bends or curves. Vertical lines run from top to bottom, like a corner of a wall from the floor to the ceiling [|]. Horizontal lines go left to right, just like the horizon [___]. A slanted line is not horizontal or vertical [/], and an angled line connects two slanted lines to make an angle [<]. Curvy, or curly, lines bend in smooth ways and express movement [~ ~]. Lines can be used in art to show perspective. Imagine standing on railroad tracks. The two slanted lines that start wide at your feet get narrower as they go farther

away. Drawing lines that are slanted like that can give the appearance of distance. Many artists start their drawing with just lines. Lines can also be connected to make other shapes. For instance, a triangle is three lines with all ends connected. After I design shapes, then I fill them in with color. This makes the drawing more interesting.

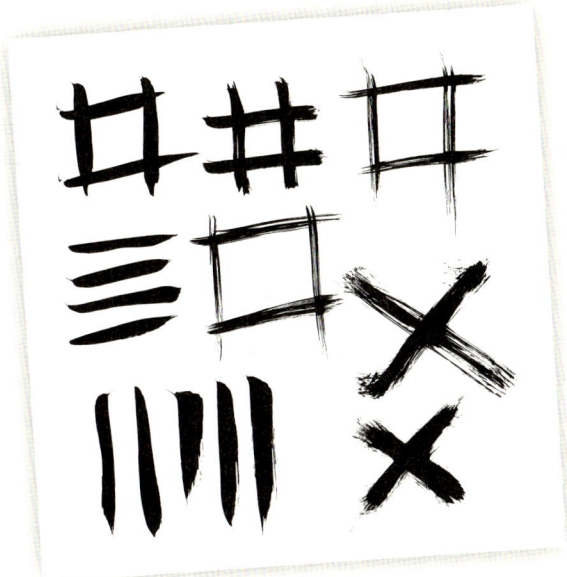

Words to Know

appearance   the way something seems or looks

basically   in the most important ways

connect   to join two or more things together

distance   the measure of space between things or places

horizontal   flat and level; straight to the ground (↔ **vertical**)

perspective   a way of showing objects on the flat surface of a picture so that they seem the correct size and distance from one another

slanted   being at a leaning or tilting angle

smooth   not rough; even

Comprehension Check-UP

A **Write the best answer.** `for NEAT`

1. What is the topic of the article?

_____

2. What kind of line has no bends or curves?

_____

B **Check whether the following statements are true or false.**

1. Lines can be very thick or very thin.   True ☐ False ☐

2. Lines that run from right to left are called vertical lines.   True ☐ False ☐

3. Perspective is conveyed by using curvy lines.   True ☐ False ☐

C **Read and choose the best answers.**

1. Which of the following lines best express movement?
   a. slanted lines   b. straight lines   c. horizontal lines   d. curly lines

2. Which of the following does NOT consist of lines?
   a. a curve   b. a point   c. an angle   d. a triangle

3. What allows a painting to give the appearance of depth and distance?
   a. Running the line from the floor to the ceiling
   b. Connecting two straight lines to form an angle
   c. After making a triangle, filling it in with color
   d. At least two slanted lines that narrow as they rise

4. Which of the following is true? `for NEAT`
   a. Some slanted lines are horizontal.
   b. Lines are not important for drawing.
   c. Triangles can have vertical lines.
   d. A circle is one curvy line.

Word Power-UP

A **Choose the best words to fill in the blanks.**

1. The cave tunnel became so _____ that they had to get on their knees and crawl.

    a. wide   b. narrow   c. connected   d. straight

2. She has a habit of straightening any _____ pictures that she sees.

    a. bending   b. horizontal   c. bottom   d. slanted

3. I don't like this _____, so would you mind changing the channel?

    a. show   b. start   c. point   d. wall

4. As punishment, the teacher made the student sit in the _____ of the classroom.

    a. track   b. line   c. corner   d. bottom

B **Complete each analogy using the best word from the right side.**

1. Vertical is to standing as _____ is to lying.   triangle   horizontal   slanted

2. Recipes are to food as _____ are to appliances.   express   appearance   directions

3. Crunchy is to snack as _____ is to ice cream.   smooth   curvy   shapes

4. The _____ are to transportation as telephone lines are to communication.

    movements   connections   railroads

C **Note the highlighted word in each selection. Then find and underline its synonym.**

1. I didn't like the looks of that cafe. Its appearance was too dirty for me.

2. The project is basically finished. Essentially, all the major problems have been solved.

3. Do you know the game connect the dots? Draw a line joining the points to find a picture.

4. We must watch our actions when near the snake. Any sudden movements could anger it.

Sum UP! Review & Finalize

Step 1. Summarizing

Fill in the blanks using words from the box below.

Lines are among the most basic _____ of artists. Using different kinds of lines an artist can _____ almost any object. The most basic line is a straight line, running either vertically or _____. _____ can be expressed by using curvy lines. Another important artistic method uses two slanted lines that _____ as they go up. Done well, this will give a realistic _____ of perspective. Connecting lines in different _____ create different shapes.

▪ horizontally	▪ movement	▪ narrow	▪ patterns
▪ represent	▪ sense	▪ tools	

Step 2. Composition for NEAT

How can an artist use lines to create the sense of perspective?

UNIT 15 Different Tastes in Music

1 Warm UP!

• **Think about the following questions.**

1. Do you like the same kind of music as your parents?

2. Why do you think people have such different tastes in music?

2 Word Preview

• **Look at the pictures and fill in the blanks with a relevant word from the box below.**

_____   _____   _____   _____   _____

drum	electric guitar	saxophone	similarity	stereo

Different Tastes in Music

Reading Strategies

Identifying the author's purpose When you read a passage, you should try to identify who the author is writing for and what the purpose of writing is. For some writing, like a letter, the audience is usually one person and the purpose of the letter is focused. So the focus of the passage will be different, and readers need to recognize this.

My mother and I have one thing in common. We both like music. That's where the similarities end. Actually, we often argue about music. I guess we have different opinions about what good music is. I like music to be loud and powerful, but she gets angry when I play my stereo at full volume. She's always yelling at me to "Turn it down!" She likes classical music. Classical music is really old, and uses traditional western instruments like violins and pianos. She also likes jazz. Jazz has instruments like saxophones and trumpets, and has a lot of improvisation. My kind of music is hip-hop, rock, and punk. Hip-hop singers say rhymes, which is more like saying poetry than singing. These rhymes are usually "rapped" over a background beat. Rock is based around the electric guitar and a fast drum beat. Punk music is similar to rock, but faster and rougher. The

punk singer usually yells her lyrics more than sings. My mother thinks that punk just sounds like loud noise. It gives me energy, but it gives her a headache. On the other hand, her music helps her to relax, but makes me bored. I guess we'll never agree on what music to listen to.

Words to Know

improvisation   a performance in which a performer invents words or musical notes without planning or practice

instrument   an object used for producing music, such as a piano

lyric   the words of a song; relating to poetry

rhyme   a word that ends with the same sound as another word. "Hop" and "stop" are rhymes for "mop."

rough   not gentle; not completely finished

traditional   related to cultural customs that have continued in similar ways for many generations

Phrases to Know

have something in common   to have the same interests or opinions as someone else

turn down   to reduce the level of sound or heat that a machine produces (↔ **turn up**)

Comprehension Check-UP

A Write the best answer. for NEAT

1. What is the topic of the article?

   _____

2. What does the speaker and her mother have in common?

   _____

B Check whether the following statements are true or false.

1. Classical music is known for its improvisation.   True ☐   False ☐

2. The speaker finds her mother's music boring.   True ☐   False ☐

3. The mother enjoys loud music.   True ☐   False ☐

C Read and choose the best answers.

1. Which of the following sing in a way that is more like saying poetry?

   a. jazz singers   b. hip-hop rappers   c. rock singers   d. punk rockers

2. Which of the following is NOT a way that the mother feels about her daughter's music?

   a. It sounds like noise.   b. It is too loud.

   c. It causes headaches.   d. It is relaxing

3. How is punk music different from rock?

   a. Rock is more improvisational and creative than punk.

   b. Punk is rougher, faster, and involves more yelling than singing.

   c. Rock is less annoying to the speaker's mother.

   d. Punk music sounds like noise, while rock is based on guitars and drums.

4. Which of the following is true? for NEAT

   a. Hip-hop is older than punk music.

   b. The mother only enjoys classical music.

   c. Most of the famous classical composers are not alive anymore.

   d. While they disagree sometimes, music brings the family together.

96

Word Power-UP

A Choose the best words to fill in the blanks.

1. Gina _____ when her brother broke her mp3 player.
   a. agreed   b. turned up   c. argued   d. got angry

2. Sarah asked Paul to _____ the radio because she couldn't hear the program.
   a. loud   b. turn up   c. fill   d. beat

3. I thought the concert would be exciting, but after the first ten minutes I got _____ and left.
   a. energy   b. relaxed   c. traditional   d. bored

4. Knowing some of the _____ of a painter can help you to appreciate her art better.
   a. energy   b. background   c. improvisation   d. similarities

B Complete each analogy using the best word from the right side.

1. Repetition is to tradition as originality is to _____.

   improvisation   jazz   poetry

2. Massage is to _____ as tickling is to laughter.   relaxation   powerful   headache

3. Brightness is to light as _____ is to sound.   beat   loud   volume

4. Michael Jackson is to pop music as the Beatles are to _____.

   electric guitars   rock   instruments

C Note the highlighted word in each selection. Then find and underline its synonym.

1. The paper is acceptable as a rough version, but it is still too unrefined to be published.

2. My favorite part of this album are the lyrics. They have such a wonderful way with words.

3. The keyboardist has trouble catching up with the rhythm. Maybe the beat is too complex.

4. We needed a CD player for this presentation, so I brought my stereo from home.

Step 1. Summarizing

Fill in the blanks using words from the box below.

People always ask me about my _____ genre of music. "What do you like? Jazz, _____, hip-hop, classical?" At first I used to think that I liked all rock music and hated all country music. But the _____ is, in every style of music there are good and bad songs. One day I heard a country song that I did enjoy, and that opened up a whole new genre to _____. Just because I enjoy some country music doesn't mean I like all country music. Even my favorite musician in the world will occasionally _____ a song that I don't like. So I guess my point is that every _____ there has both good music and bad music. My favorite music is good music.

▪ explore	▪ genre	▪ favorite
▪ truth	▪ make	▪ punk

Step 2. Composition for NEAT

How is your musical taste different from that of your parents?

UNIT 16 Is Volleyball Better Than Baseball?

1 Warm UP!

- **Think about the following questions.**
  1. What is your favorite sport?
  2. Why do you think sports are so popular?

2 Word Preview

- **Look at the pictures and fill in the blanks with a relevant word from the box below.**

_____ _____ _____ _____ _____

| baseball | basketball | handball | tennis | volleyball |

Is Volleyball Better Than Baseball?

Track 16

Reading Strategies

Understanding attitude & mood Attitude is a reflection of how the author feels about a topic. By choosing a certain attitude, the author informs you of his or her attitude toward a topic. Mood is the overall feelings of a story. It can be created by the setting, or where the story takes place. Many different words have almost same meaning, yet each may create a slightly different mood.

Dear diary,

I'm confused! You know how much I love baseball. I write about it nearly every day! But today at school we played another game called volleyball. It was really great! The net is very high and it is a bit difficult, but I'm sure with practice I can become a good player. I really like the fact that the game seems to be a mixture of tennis, baseball, handball, and basketball — and because it is an indoor game I can play even if it is raining. My teacher said that nearly 800 million people play it each week, making it one of the world's most popular sports! I read on the Internet that William G. Morgan invented it in 1895.

Of course, nothing can replace baseball totally! I learned today about

'USA Baseball,' which is the organization in the USA that was founded in 1978 and runs amateur baseball competitions. It has a huge job! It not only organizes high school and college teams but it also fields the USA Baseball International team in exhibition matches both in the US and internationally against teams like Korea, Japan and Canada. It also organizes the USA Junior Olympic Baseball Championships and fields the under-16 and under-18 teams. Wow!

So now I'm not sure which I like the most... what should I do?

Comprehension Check-UP

A Write the best answer. [for NEAT]

1. What is the topic?

_____

2. Which sport does the writer prefer?

_____

B Check whether the following statements are true or false.

1. Volleyball was invented in 1895.   True ☐   False ☐

2. The writer has played volleyball for a long time.   True ☐   False ☐

3. USA Baseball was founded by William G. Morgan.   True ☐   False ☐

C Read and choose the best answers.

1. Which of the following tasks does USA Baseball NOT do?

   a. Manages professional leagues   b. Runs international competitions

   c. Fields under-18 and under-16 teams   d. Organizes high school baseball teams

2. Which of the following is an advantage that volleyball has over baseball?

   a. Baseball cannot be totally replaced.

   b. There are many amateur teams and competitions.

   c. It is one of the world's most popular sports.

   d. It can be played indoors during poor weather.

3. According to the writer, what is difficult about volleyball?

   a. It is too much a mixture of other sports.   b. So many people play it.

   c. The net is so high.   d. It doesn't have large organizations.

4. Which of the following is true? [for NEAT]

   a. The writer writes about volleyball very often.

   b. The writer is confident that he can improve in volleyball.

   c. The writer likes all sports equally.

   d. The writer decided that volleyball is better.

Word Power-UP

A Choose the best words to fill in the blanks.

1. I'm totally _____. I don't understand it.
   a. confused   b. replaced   c. excited   d. organized

2. She is a _____ girl in my school. Everybody likes her.
   a. poor   b. huge   c. difficult   d. popular

3. The new design will _____ all old models.
   a. replace   b. place   c. return   d. remain

4. Her family _____ the college in 1875.
   a. pressed   b. founded   c. recalled   d. turned

B Complete each analogy using the best word from the right side.

1. _____ is to sport as rap is to music.   Volleyball Piano Song

2. Teacher is to teach as _____ is to play.   engineer player swimmer

3. _____ is to ceiling as outdoors is sky.   Indoors Door Window

4. _____ is to inexperience as professional is to experience.

                                                       Amateur Expert Volunteer

C Note the highlighted word in each selection. Then find and underline its synonym.

1. The city is a mixture of old and new buildings. You can feel the combination of old and new.

2. Who invented the telephone? Alexander Graham Bell created the first telephone.

3. Workers are not allowed to organize unions. Despite this, they are trying to form one.

4. Their new house is huge. Can you believe how large it is?

 **Step 1. Summarizing**

Fill in the blanks using words from the box below.

Almost everyone has heard of sports superstars such as David Beckham and Michael Jordan, but few people could name any _____ volleyball players. Despite its _____ of media attention, volleyball is one of the most _____ sports for people to play. Why is volleyball so popular? It has _____ of many other sports, which makes it familiar and exciting. It is quite easy to set up; the only equipment needed is a _____ and a ball. Also, it can be played outside on grass or _____, or can be played indoors during any kind of _____. If volleyball is this popular, one has to wonder when will the first volleyball athlete become a superstar.

• elements	• lack	• net	• popular
• professional	• sand	• weather	

Step 2. Composition `for NEAT`

Do you prefer watching professional athletes compete or playing sports yourself?